This Moon Looms For You

Nevaeh Frazee

Copyright © 2018 Nevaeh Frazee

All rights reserved.

ISBN-13: 978-0-578-47857-9

For those who have wronged me. This book is not for you.
For those in a time of need. This is all for you.

ACKNOWLEDGEMENTS

To my mother and my father — the strongest people I have ever known.
To my sister, whose support has consistently lifted me up.
To my friends who have never failed to enlighten my world.
To Tyler, who helped me create the wonderful masterpiece of this cover.
To SWMT—my second family— whose opportunities have given me the confidence to be the person I am today.

And to you. Thank you for the love and support. You have made this all possible.

XO,
Nevaeh

These
These are the hours we count
From the darkest light
To the sleepy sun rising
We find crucial
Every minute of raging thoughts
And creative dreams
To form into realities

These hours we count
By the second
Whether time enlightens us
Or frightens us
Our souls all become one
Under the looming moon
As it attentively dawns upon our awakened minds

I hope these moments
And words
Will bring your thoughts
To clarity and sanction
During these fragile times

~ *N. f.*

12 : 0 0 a. m.

Consent should be mutual
Consent does not mean
Coming on to you, when I was not
In a capable mindset of doing so
As the blurry images of him set into my eyelids
I knew what we did
And I knew in my heart
I did not want that

Do you hear me?

I did **not** consent
I did **not** want that
And now you're blaming me?
It was my body
And you took advantage of me
I did **not** consent
    —Colorado Revised Statues Sections 12-3-402: Sexual Assault

$\sim N.\,f.$

I don't think you could comprehend
The trauma you caused me
All the nights
That were an insomniac nightmare
Because of your lies
And all of my care and love
Laid to waste
I don't think you could comprehend
The damage I've suffered
At the hands of your ignorance

~ N. f.

I look beyond
Behind them is a stranger
Like looking into the eyes of recognition
But incomprehensible registers their face
I soundly cross to them—
To the edge I will stand
Reach for you against the wind
Hovering my fingers—
Strange how the fickle of light warmth still lingers
Even into the deepest of graves

$\sim N.f.$

Love a poet
They will make you immortal
But don't break a poet
They'll leave no surface unturned
They'll try to write the world away
With a pen of tears and a heart full
Of you

~ *N. f.*

When you broke up with me
You held my hands and said
> *We'll work through this. We can be friends*
I frowned and asked you
> *Will it ever be the same?*

But it never would have been, I know
I was holding hands with someone
I thought was going to last
To try everything in their power to persevere

But instead I was grasping you,
A friend, that too easily slipped away
From being a lover

~ N. f.

I am guilty
Of an addiction
Of trust, of lust
Of letting you in

~ N. f.

As easily as I came into your life
I could be wiped away from it as well
It's clear to me that I was nothing
But a fantasy of your craziest dreams
And when reality crept up on you
I was nothing more
Than your unfinished story

~ N. f.

This is what happens
To a girl when she
Turns broken bones
Into love poetry

When she becomes the one thing
He told her she'd
Never be:
    Shattered

~ N. f.

Who was she? I asked
You laughed. *Just a friend. We just talk*

I shook away the concern and relieved a smile

Weeks later, I held a box
With a beautiful gift and asked

Can you come over? I have a surprise
It was our anniversary, and you told me
I can't. I'm with a friend
With her?
Yeah

I laid the box next to me
And still brushed away the concern
But I was still worried,
And something in me wouldn't
Let it rest

You severed our relationship
And I wanted to talk, but you said

I can't, I'm with a friend
With her?
Yeah, don't be mad

But I am
I am infuriated
Because I knew it all along
I just didn't want it to be true

~ N. f.

Another child laid under the grass
Another bloody headline
They should make teachers carry guns
They say
They should hire more security
They comment
They should check student's bags
They circle the administration
How could we have known this was going to happen?
They kiss their children's foreheads
Afraid, for the last time,
Should we have to plan for the worst?
Should I have to plan to barricade myself
Against a parade of gunshots
Inside a building that should be safe?
Should I have to call my family
And whisper to them I love them
For the final time?
How many graves will we have to dig up
In order for the world to wake up?
Teachers should not have to carry guns,
And guns should not be stripped from the free,
But how many children need to be buried
For more regulations to be passed
And for our schools
To stop becoming a funeral?

~ N. f.

It hurts me to say,
But I loved you, and I'm sorry if you can't take
The truth, not because it's true,
But because it hurts

~ *N. f.*

My dear
So hungover from tears
He grabbed your hand
And told you he didn't love you
Like he use to
Those were the words
That shattered your universe
Because as he held you,
His skin so cold and unadoring,
Your only wish was to feel something
Anything, to remind you
Of all the things he did to you
You, you, you
The shoulder he let you cry on
The tear stains
Embedded in the cotton weaves
So tight, so deep,
Maybe enough to not make him leave
You at the door with only a goodbye
Refraining from an *I love you*,
As if he could see the sorrow in your eyes
And still chose to drive away

~ N. f.

Desolation has long since decorated the state
　Complete and utter human touch erased
　　No other than the heart itself destroyed

~ N. f.

They say I'm *easy*
Like a hunt
To take their turns
Prodding at my wounds
Getting me vulnerable
And ravaging like wolves
For my carcass
I think this is idiotic
Because all I've even given was my heart
And I am not *easy* to obtain
I am not a figure of curves
Anyone can snag
Or a test for how far they can
Cross my boundaries
And I am **sick** of my confidence
In the way my body dips and twists
Being mistaken for
She asked for it
I am a human
Not a game for the dogs
   —I am more than a body

$\sim N.f.$

The vacant sides of me are all porous and blisters
Maybe at night I just forget to sleep
The nightmares are in my life,
Dreams when I'm slumbering
Give your all into my hands
And when nothing's left
I will destroy my forest's roots to water yours
And disembark my veins for you

Maybe what I weep for
Is not my mourning death
But simply the fact you never appeared
At the funeral
That your name was never signed
Beneath my will
Yet in my hollow bones
Your spirit lies and lingers
In the porous holes, deep in these blazing blisters

~ N. f.

And it burns
Everywhere your fingers traced
Your touch grazing off layers of me
Yet not scalding from a blade
Trying to take portions of my skin
But flaking flesh in holes I cannot see
Wounds I have yet to feel
Because I put my universe into your hands
And they *shook*

I observe these scars peeling open,
For I have too much heart to carry
My chest yet again heavy
Brusing, beckoning, bleeding
Falters I continue to make

My own stitches I rip out
To let new rich poisons seep in
When you look away
With panning annoyance
I find myself swinging
In the eyes of someone
Who falters, yet falters
At the risk of others

He has let me go
And so must I
Mend these burns

~ N. f.

Grow a flower for me when you leave, my love
So I know you came

~ N. f.

I'm not feeling heartbroken, really
I'm feeling broken
For the loveless skeleton
That I have become

~ N. f.

I've watched my heart fall
From the shelf a hundred times
And peel the glassy pieces
With my fingernails
Off the tile floor only
To place them back on rotting wood
Where no flowers bloom
I scourge excuses to make
For the lack of sunlight—
Sadly I am at loss for how to repose
Them out of the shade—
I am broken, weltering leaves
But maybe one day
I can teach myself
How to breathe
And piece
The damage back
To wholesome bliss

~ N. f.

My demons are problems
That I dress up in phrases
Or pages
Perhaps even novels
Of everything that should repel them
But they travel back
They always do
I don't want theme here—
They've never had a welcome stay

~ N. f.

Sparks float from my skin
Of embers and fire
That burn my soul alive
In a withering, concaving devastation

~ N. f.

The frozen handles on the clock
Keep me isolated
With frozen cheeks that keep melting
Droplets onto the ankles of my feet
I cradle the sweatshirt as if it were a lifeline
But it isn't strong enough
To keep me afloat
Not this time
Text bubbles surface the icy waters
In hopes, spitefully hopeful,
For a better place
Remorse leaking
Into pools of blue
They stain so much tissue of my soul
That is capable of deepening into oceans
The hour is so young
For crumbling lips
Too late for *I love you*
Too young for *I'm sorry*
And so sinking down I go
Down, down, drown
My heart goes
Once more

$\sim N.f.$

Let's play a game, sweetheart
Games were what you enjoyed
But my heart was no game
You knew this
Yet you played with it anyways

~ N. f.

I long for something
To make the stars
Shine bright again

~ N. f.

You lied
And lies are all I've known
For you left me staring into the dark
   —Lonesome is not a state of mind I wish to stay in

$\sim N.f.$

Tell me how
To unravel all of my love
For you
(For it was so easy for you
Maybe you can teach me)

~N. f.

1 : 0 0 a.m.

Tell me how

To unravel all of my love
For you

Ask yourself this,
What profit of relations will become of this?
If not for selfish reasons nor movement—
A conveying of emotion
We'll hang in thin air, lips parted sparingly
Upon a dark kiss
Masked by the holy, take your hand
In my own
A chapel of crystal and bone
In a single free, fleeting motion,
Abiding blindly to each other in three, two…

But what becomes a vase caressing the white rose?
No water, no sun, solitary and left alone?
If selfish doesn't apply, your sparing breaths fire
Your lungs will burn, your neck will grow tired
From the weight of the burden you carry
Parted lips, I scream *liar, liar liar!*

~ N. f.

1:11
Piano soft in my ear
Dressing flesh wounds that are neither agonizing
Nor real, yet under my breasts
Pain is eminent here
Alas, I have no broken ribs
But at 1:11, I am only skin
And skin grafts will cover only but lesions
For when I tide and rise high
Suffrage and drowning awakens in my deletion
My absence is noteworthy
All I am is pure energy and life
At 1:11 I can't mirror or shelter myself
There isn't a seclusion I can hide behind
I long for a piano
Grander than a lake, deeper than the ocean
Delicate as the rain, powerful as the thunder
Every word lost in its silence wonderfully broken
With the top exposed, so I don't feel alone
And I will sit eloquently on the black stool
Child, take my hand and show me everything
I've wanted to say; allow me to choose
A song we can dance to together
Under the heart of my fairy lights
At 1:11 in the morning
Allow us to play the agony of darkness
Into a sovereign light

$$\sim N.f.$$

(Do you ever wonder what the world could become
At 1:11?)

I can feel the universe
Inside of me
Porous through my ribs
Bleeding cosmo dust
Breathing
Solar winds
I carve stars in the margins of my heart
The ones they say I breathe,
I bleed,
I am weak because I don't understand the universe,
But darling,
Maybe the universe doesn't understand me

~ N. f.

I am the agonizing fear struck in the hearts of young men
The hope, the light after eternal darkness,
The failure after failure, then rewarding success
An entire world bottled into a singular girl
With the power to commend fleets of soldiers
The ability to control—
But this isn't true power
Instead I wish to channel the rain to fall when I please
Or to captivate the snow under a blue moon
The world to revolve not 'round me
But a legacy to bathe in the limelight

And the progenies—oh the ancestors as to the progenies
Which are we?
If we live to see our children become ancestors
Enlighten me, what does that make of us?
I can become all I imagine, distilled in the blood works
Of a future only I may reach
If I pass tomorrow, will poetry be my legacy?
Can satisfaction ever reach you if you know at the
Last moment you will pass on with your symphony?
And if why not spoken these words
Will a strength of light never be received?
To tell me I am that with all the power in the world
I am everything, and nothing,
Why not said after I called out
That while timelines are rather short
It's what we should perceive our lives to be?

~ N. f.

I've seen thing no one else believes
I feel things that are different from what everyone sees

~ N. f.

Drowsy little thing
You let your hips sway
To the floods of moonlight
Swerving to the waves
It remembers the beach
You never went to,
But daydreamed you'd always reach
Darlings rocked between the clammy bodes of music
You rocked to the clasps
Of warm fingers, something
Made you roll your shoulders
Stand straight, sigh
The shiver of your spine
Under cold rumbles of water
You remember the way
His fingertips lacing tunes of his own
To the instrument of your skin
Half believing the man next to you
Was really him
Am **I** in love?
Am I in love?
In love?
If only you knew

~ N. f.

Happy new year
You wished me from across the street
I didn't look up
My feet wouldn't budge from the pavement
Did you hear me?
I heard you, but I feel invisible
I nod, gaze up to your face in the streetlight
And as a tear spills down my cheek,
Silent, I turn away from you
I couldn't be near you
I couldn't stand the thought of you
Being in my life
After all this time of ignoring me
And calling me crazy
I couldn't go into the new year
With someone like you
Consistently in the back of my mind
Taking away from the "new" part of the year

~ N. f.

We've gathered more about each other
Than poetry has been spoken
To describe the ways
How you remind me I'm alive
You gave me everything—
But your actions were short of reach
My spirit cannot reconcile itself
With the traces of her left on your lips

~ N. f.

Of miles across
This carpet carries fog
Of which only your eyes pierce through
I can see the ocean
Behind your blue eyes
Mine, too,
Reflect what yours do,
The trickle of acid
Down the inferior slant of your throat
Burning your soul
Sizzling and crackling fireworks
And I only wish to give the aloe of my smile
To the seared scars of your heart

~ N. f.

I find it ironic
That the stories
And the poetry
I pile in here
My book—my heart—
Will never be enough for you to hear
As loud as I am scribbling down
These raging thoughts
I will never be enough for you
It hurts enough already
To be loved only part way

~ N. f.

I still love you
But what would that change?
What could possibly bring the past
From the graveyard,
And arise again the wisps of young
Laughter
An old love,
As a floating ghost crippling in the sun
What say you at the end of the day,
In the morn'
Morbid with the scars of life
And riddled with the moon?
What say you?

$\sim N.f.$

Where did you go
When I needed you the most?
And why did you leave
When you needed me, too?

~ *N. f.*

It takes two to dance together
To joke in the morning
To nourish and heal
Hands need snow to catch
Doors need frames—
You can have two hinges,
But not two ways to swing
And like all of these
A book needs its pages
Much like this book, it will become
Soiled, crippled and meshed
Love worn out the spine
Lines upon underlines
But not two endings

~ N. f.

I hate you
Because you stubbornly won't
Leave my life
And you know this
Yet you continuously
Spiral this pain more and more
Deep into my veins
Spiraling into something
More than I just can't bear to handle
I want you
And I hope you treat her well
Make her smile in all of the ways
That you made me

~ N. f.

Oh, how the chandelier
Swung at the midnight strike
How the desolated state
Grew alive at the sound
Of static rumbling across the prairie
And sunk deep beneath the weeds
Retrogressing back to the plundering seas
No organized rows of sky scrapers
Could be large enough borders
To keep our other halves
Weltering from one another
Even during storms,
The city will continue to sway with
Arrogant proportion,
The size of charm unfathomable
The weak will permeate the bold
The world will gather as a whole being
Of other lonely halves
Yearning for someone bound to be
Half way across the city
With the morning growing warm
The static moves on
Oh, how life wards soundly on

$\sim N. f.$

I'm sorry
    For the sparkle I dissipated
        I have never really seen
This side of love
    But there is no winning against someone
        That has already made their mind up

$$\sim N.f.$$

I can still retrace my skin
And remember where you saved your prints
Embedded in the soft layers
Iron casted into my veins
From that necklace
Fiber glass pockets
Loomed through the heart of my collarbone
When your lips parted,
My ears fed from your split tongue
Licked up of venomous drippings
I absorbed each and every laced up satire
Pinned with accessories of compliments
And draped eloquently in velvet lies

~N. f.

The night grows cold
When you are missing

Every time you leave
It's like you take a piece of my lungs

It's like every time you leave
I'm finding it harder to close my eyes

It's like every time you leave
I can't dream knowing you're not mine

From the time we vow
To the ends of our day

We promised to kindle our flame
And I shall return

Yes, I will, and always
Still return to our vow

Kindling what's left
Please, let us collide, and let me show you

The damage that has been done
Don't forget those midnights

Don't you dare abandon me to the storm

$\sim N.f.$

Why can't you bleed out already
All these scars
And you could not slip out with them
After all this time
Why could you not trickle down the handles
And ring and ring, and ring away
From the folds of my soul

~ N. f.

Oh quiet leader,
He who stalks amongst the aspen trees
Regal and tall, bowed with ancient bones
What makes the sky breathe?
If mind be defined by false truth
It must derail in the face of reality
The truth can be a monster
Who lies
In the face of the fat moon
Who lays awake, silently

~ N. f.

I still recall the first moment with you
As if it were only yesterday
I continue to hang onto it
As if it could happen again tomorrow

~ N. f.

The wind blowing down
From the open top of his car
Whisked up blunt cologne
And hundreds of adventures
Present in the front seats
We looked up to watercolor clouds
And bright stars
Brushing the cold of the night
Away with the warmth of the heater
As it sank deep within us
The stars begged me to lean over
To hold him
The leather seat a tight constraint
So in this swirl of ice and fire
To bear these solemn thoughts
To keep still, ever so beckoning
To the cricket's cries
I could see it in his eyes—
The emptiness that kills

~N. f.

To him
He who lingers
In the chain of my collar bone
And basks in the strands of my hair
To whisper little lies and press his bloody lips
To the back of my lobe
A seam to the brooks of venom
Investing in my veins

~ N. f.

I, the trophy,
That should be off the mantle,
Have these scars
That are too disturbing to ignore
I am too dismantled
By his crucifying hands
And mangled into the back of his
Closet, bones scathing from my muscles obscurely
Too immobile
I clench my teeth with fire
For letting myself become a target
Mistaking it
For his love

~ *N. f.*

I continue to embody a lust
For ache
Romanticize my own torment
And too often
My heart is so open,
Often so forgiving,
I let it stretch thin
I gave him a chance
To prove them incorrect
And find wholeness in his breath
But as I write this
He has not crossed my presence
In hours
I'm writing poetry to cope
Because I'm familiar with these
Habitual tendencies—
So copious and repetitive
That I can even make out
How he's running his fingers through
Her hair
That instead should be in mine

~ N. f.

Why don't you listen to anyone?

Darling, you don't understand
How hard I love

How hard I fall for them

~ N. f.

2 : 0 0 a. m.

Darling, you don't understand

How hard I love

They tell me to *say goodbye*
But I just can't
I just can't, and I chase him as
He pulls away
I cling to his shirt like a hawk
To rise me from this world
And I fall as if it shocked me

Well,
It did.

And the world shook as I hit it
The ground reverberated as I lay silent
Wounded, watching the silhouette of his wings
His shadow casted down upon me
And all I could do was watch an
I love you
Fade away
    — *Maybe those wings aren't from an angel*

~ N. f.

Your eyes speak of dreams
But the whiskey whispers devils
That are always ill-consuming

~ N. f.

Sometimes I wonder
If you think about
The way I kissed you
And if the image remains
Glued in your mind
For the rest of the night

~ *N. f.*

Don't you dare run your hands
Through your hair
If you tempt me
I won't be able
To forgive
Myself

~ N. f.

Breathe in
    And out
And in
    And the cycle repeats
Again and again

~ N. f.

Poetry is not only the story—
It is the beginning of everything
I am only a vessel
Aloft waters of clocks and
The horizon a long blur as
Rocking through the icy sea and I'm
Carrying the soft spoken songs of quiet doves
I shine for thee
With all the instruments in the world
It's hard as is to compose a symphony
Yet I shall look on
Paper my raft, pencil my oar
I sail, my eyes fixed on the lazy horizon
Often painting the stars and sunrise
Little of the shore

~ N. f.

I wish I possessed the capability
To conjure up a projection
Of the colors your eyes turn
When the corners of your lips
Rise

I want to contort the idea
Wet cheeks are the poster child
For crying
By crossing out *sad*
And writing next to it *emotion*

For every cloud
I pray to replicate the fabrication
Of amber panels
Swallowed by the haze of the day

I seek someone to tell me
I am no wall sentences
Just bounce from
Or a spokesmodel
That cannot hear

I wish so much more
Than a single plane
Of endless lines —symmetrical they are—
But they are countlessly filled with
Doubts
And a wish for more eyes
I can gaze into

~ N. f.

Have I not been honest
with you?

~ N. f.

I'm sorry
To the tears in your heart
I'm sorry for what you felt
And the words that spoke to you so profoundly
I must've made you drive
Toward the edge of insanity
Where your heart
Just stopped beating
Before my very sight

~ N. f.

In the time
That you struggle to hang onto
The divot of my waist
Your lips cannot reach me
Frantically, you lurk for
Any part of me to cling to
But catch you will nothing

~ *N. f.*

We all believe love is the most vital thing
As if we could grasp it and cast
It all into the night
When we break

~ N. f.

You tried to hold me
Like a doll
And I do not need you
To fiddle with my stitches
And my nails
Anymore than you already have

~ N. f.

If my strength as a woman
To tell you when you have misdemeanor
Turns you off, then you don't deserve
To be in a relationship
If you think a woman telling you
How you took advantage of her body
Would *chase guys away*,
And I should keep my mouth shut
I am disgusted you believe
Women are going to respect you—
Someone who tells women
To be quiet about their assault
　　— *You're not a real man*

~ N. f.

There's a line between a life and a lie
A common place where we all come across
And the eyes you have set aside for me
I cannot love
There's too much dream to paint the reality
The wine in my veins spills vicariously
You're nothing short of deserving love,
Yet clearly I am nothing worth to you, I apologize

~ N. f.

If we take the labels off
Throw them into the sea, see them as words
As vowels and constants become foreign to our ears
Would this world finally become equal?
Unlabeled equality,
But even that name we ravish
It's no wonder after all this time,
I cannot love you so
Because our lives are bubbling concepts
In a bobbing sea we continue to ponder

~ *N. f.*

He told me words
As simple
And as complicated
As that

~ N. f.

His words formed wings
Of light to flutter in my lungs
And pebbles to gather
In the chambers of my vessels
These words were keen
In making sure my lips
Would grow tired
And tremble with ache
For I curled them for so long

But your words were fish hooks
That in theory were promising, but in turn
Made me numb
   —Remind yourself to listen carefully

~ N. f.

Words are not meant
To burn
I don't like the way
They've been branded
On the backs of my lids
Because it forms this script
I must recite

~ *N. f.*

The heart's recollection of time
Has little motive to how it feels
It will continue to beat, to live,
For someone as long as it desires
And does not return what it owns
Easily
    —My heart is beautifully stubborn

$\sim$ N. f.

You carry these entanglements
As dressings, bands and bedazzlements
For you hum a sweet lullaby
Tuning down these instruments

~ N. f.

I've spent quiet hours
Doing seemingly important work
That to him is the equivalent
Of staring up a wall
What he never unveiled
Was his scarf of insecurity
Ambled and rosed up
For my work is the equivalent
To passing bills and winning awards
It's what makes you feel alive that's worth it all
I sorrow him
Because he has yet to find
Something that makes him quiver
In the middle of the night
By just uttering words
Or breathing in the presence
Of the pure, unrequited passion
That I have found
Even if it is behind closed doors,
He will never understand
But perhaps will
At the moment I crack them open to the world

~ N. f.

The world has pressed me so hard
On all of the things I have ever loved
Judged for my passions,
I've learned numbness
In these years and years
I still wish I could carry myself away from it all
The fake laughs, the phony smiles,
I could carry them all
But they drown out
Into the deepest of ocean
In the crack of the morn'

~ N. f.

Give me full release
Give me sweet dreams for when I sleep

~ N. f.

The bipolar in my winters
Is very drastic
For the winds are sharp
The trees shed their leaves
Blanket the pavement with
Plethoras of dried, shriveled inklings
Of the moments that decompose
For the children to dive into
How can beauty derive from Death,
Or so, Death reconcile a Memory?
The memory are the trees
And so they grow and shed
Both Beauty and Death
Blinding, unkempt catastrophe
They continuously bloom
Into gardens of wanderlust
Find sanctuary underneath the shadows
Casted eloquently amongst the grown
Forgetful of its temporary placement
This forgetfulness is why
My winters are the most bitter
Amongst all others

N. f.

3 : 0 0 a. m.

Find sanctuary underneath the shadows

If only you dreamed
    Golden girl
Forever to gleam
    Sunny girl
     His eyes
Stretched as marvelous
As the canvassing sea
He'll never truly know
    The golden girl
      Staring
    A subtle dream

~ N. f.

Premature
Love has been labeled in so many ways
However this was the one
That remains glued to my tongue
The early onset of giving oneself
Fully to another
Has been counteracted
By the superficial reason
That we were premature

$\sim N.f.$

How can you perform an exorcism
On a ghost
That refuses to vanish?

~ *N. f.*

She is a tarnishing dye, makes you turn green
Her blindness drives her, dives her
Plunging her to the sea
She's head first in poison, and arms out to the flames
And she will not rest before them this night

$\sim N.f.$

Meagerly, mediocrely,
We must abide to our secret consents
Even with knowledge of others,
We might be blinded ourselves

                              ~ N. f.

If you ask yourself
If one, or two, or ten of these works
Are about you,
Do not ask
If you feel strongly connected
And these words touch you so close
Your intuition might be right
However, do not ask,
Because these are not meant for you
No ill-manner should sprout to taint
What we once had
These words are for me,
And for them—
All who have ever felt alone
Without sanction or someone to
Confide with
This is their sanctuary
Not your memorial

~ N. f.

I think we're all
A little tired
A little sick
And a little in love

~ *N. f.*

My love,
You understand my pain
Almost as if you have lived through it with me
You clear all the right spots
You guide me from my shell
In the most loving and tender way
You fight unrequitedly
Almost relentlessly
Just for one more minute of small speech
I am at loss for
Maybe you hold onto me so tight
Because you're afraid of losing sight
But with all my power, my love,
I will try to heal your pain
As equally as you understand mine

~ N. f.

I wish there was an elixir or potion
That could carry all the care I have
To your heart
And diffuse it
To every waiting cell
So every inch of you could learn
The feelings I give so strongly
Are a real, untainted
Pure concentrate
Of my heart and lungs—
And the extract of my smile
To line the backs of your lids
So you'll never miss it—
The trimming of my eyes
That could show you the wonder
I see swimming through your soul
With this magic
I'd be able to prove to you
That all the beauty in the world
Can still be seen with mortal eyes
Found in the most unique nooks and crannies,
In the most of unsuspecting things, it lies

$\sim N.f.$

We were a storm
Life in the eye
Chaos submerging
Everything we wrote together
Drenching the pages
Too far the ink
Bled colors of blue and black
Dripping from the corners, spreading the page
And drying with a new blotchy form
By the eye of the sun
Looking for the last
Remaining letters of incomprehension
But still recognizes the layers
Of meaning
Behind the mysterious distater
That became of us

~ N. f.

Look at me
The wind flows so fair
Brushing through my locks
Flowing down my dress
Fusing within my eyes
Look at me
And take in the woman I have
Become to encompass
For all of the beauty I possess

~ N. f.

His hands felt welcoming
The first time he held me
His fingers not elongated
But fit so well 'round my shoulder
They were the refined product
Of late night keyboards
And grand pianos

But no matter how beautiful of music
He tried to make of me,
The tune was never as sharp
Nor as clear
As we intended to compose it

My hands are little
Not small, but rather my palms
Lay flat when draped on his chest
Mine are soft spoken,
But rough from written papers
And pencil dust on my sixth finger
I have the eyes of the lake
His are the night

When we gaze upon each other
It's noticeable the night cannot shine upon a lake
Without the moon
Just like these words cannot shape
Us into perfect melodies

~ N. f.

To you, my love
While I walk down these halls
Of nothing but a hollow chest
And craving eyes
I want nothing but your smile
It's captivating
Memorizing
Tempting
But as a moth drawn to a flame
I feel my wings against the ravenous sun
As you watch from the sockets of my gaze
Hypnotized
Oh why
Do mistakes like these
Have to come from beautifully wrecking people
Like you?

~ N. f.

My love,
I pour my eyes into your hands
Hoping you could see how much I didn't
Wish for out time to cease, but I couldn't have lived
With bullet wounds in my breasts
That matched your gun
Because if we waited any longer,
I would have bled to death
Before you could have taken me down
All over again

$\sim N.f.$

I wish the stars to watch
Over your humbling body
From all harm sent your way
I wish we could take the dust off our hearts
And cast them amongst the stars
Would yours and mine sit next to each other?
Keep the other company?
Talk for infinity?
Continue our symphony as a seed
We planted in the sky to pass on
Will they fall into the lungs of other people
And search for each other again?
I solemnly believe
Pieces of our hearts and souls
Will be waiting to fall
And find love again
    —What does it mean to love with all your heart and soul?

~ N. f.

What is it you're searching for,
love?

~ N. f.

Why is the hand I own
Never called to my possession
And my name for one to swoon
A sigh, for one has no lesson
I listen delicately to the hearts
Straddled to young wilderness' sleeves
Tame, yet unkept
And place my finger
To their craving lips
For I am the wild one
And only a wish it may be

~ N. f.

When one's chest falls like mine
Mimics the good and they shall receive
All good and pure kin they wish to receive of me

~ N. f.

I know I've left my home
Instead my head for somewhere
Far unexplored
And adventure wildly
I shall go
Even in the face of fear—
A fear that no longer
Consumes me

~ N. f.

He makes my skin tingle

No.

He should make your soul
Crawl with such pleasure
A single word won't be able
To describe the rich power
It does to you

~ *N. f.*

Here, in the length of your arms
Should be your warmth
I stand with my story
Raging with passion
None dare to disturb
All those I know
Are miles across the sea
And I just ache
Bleed
Flinch
Feed
To tell you
You need to understand
Your storm is not strong enough
To take me down

~ N. f.

4 : 0 0 a. m.

Your storm is not strong enough
To take me down

The moon whispered stories hinted
Towards our youth
The love we laughed about, it heard

~ N. F.

Your blood runs sweet
As it is only natural
To love
To live
To list
To be happy
And yet is so tainted
With the thickening temptation
To criticize
To envy
To gain power
And most importantly
Become an entity
Your blood was not meant
To handle at all

~ N. f.

Become addicted to life
And I argue this
Because there is no
Stronger addiction
Because it will become a lifestyle
You will forever remain hungry for

~ N. f.

Loving another
Should not result
In the loss
Of yourself

~ *N. f.*

I'm sorry
To the next woman to come after me
The one with the real soft lips
And plush skin
I'm sorry
To those women wishing for a life of shining stars
When all he has to offer
Are dusty clouds
You are not oblivious—no, you are strong—
But his lips keep you dreaming all night long
I'm sorry
To the next woman he seizes
Even if she wanted him
His touch does not belong in those curves
And the lies he can't, and won't, admit to
I'm sorry
He only wants perfect
He craves it like a habit
But like me, she will learn soon enough
A boy like him
Isn't worth it

~ N. f.

There's a certain beauty
That fixes itself
Inside a woman
With unfinished pieces
But knows of her purpose
The soul will kindle
Every lasting flake
Gently
Tenderly
And full of love
Acknowledging
That even the unknown
Can be beautiful
And worthy
And she will grow from it

~ *N. f.*

Eyes of the atmosphere focus from afar
Love and lust, a lucid child among the stars
A milky way that's never been seen
Full of little lights watching over me
Below the wool blanket of trees
A bearded man softly sleeping
And idly next to him is one in the wake
Watching the red carps filter down the lake
Laying gently down her small, soft head
Purring, eyes closed, drifting off to bed
A little boy of four feet tall
Hoists himself up to the wall
Watching the window change the world around him
As the sunrise breaks the horizon form afar
Of the singular breath that he is
The hands bring upon him an immortal kiss
Crooning the babe, tending rocking care
Floating gently in momma's hair

$\sim N.f.$

Look closely
Her eyes will speak the truth

~ *N. f.*

On two sides of the world
The blue ocean connects
One side pulls the current closer
And the other one rests
Much like two doves
Perched upon a wire
One has flow enough
While the other continues to fly higher
Two trees sit idly
Trunk by trunk
Red and orange consumes the left
And the right blooms just enough
What astounds me the most
Is the capability both of these parallels exist
In a world of danger and chaos
Either would be missed
To choose which is the best
Is hardly a fair trade
On two sides
My left heart and my right
I will handle well
Look after both equally
And tend to them with a caring mind

$\sim N.f.$

I know how to croon the neck of a guitar
Between my palm and gently
Pick the lips of the strings
I know how to coax the metal eyes
Into singing for me
It may be softly tuned
Or of fast temper,
But I know how this soul works
Its laced deep within the frame
You cannot open the strands
Just to ask for its name
I know how to grow into one's heart
Because I've learned
How to play one
Every day
You have yet to learn
The patient mind it takes
To mend one's soul
And have failed to do so
With mine
But here, I shall continue strumming
And singing
With a whole and beautiful
Heart of my own

~ N. f.

You must know
The sun must rise
Before you admire the horizon

~ N. f.

The universe's grasp may be infinite
But I am not
— *My love*

~ *N. f.*

Out of the fresh morning
Out of singing mocking jays and blue birds
To seek a threshold beyond this evergreen nest
Beyond these staggering mountains
Take me beyond this gratified fortress
Dedicated to enclose me with the thickets of pines
I will summon a hundred spirits to march alongside
My wakening body
I will take all of my soul
Find refuge in the midst of fate
And no longer will I be reprimanded
Inside this state—no more
Shall I suffer like a caged animal
Foaming at the seams
In exchange, I will bleed wild color
In the stripes of a tiger
To everywhere I reach

~ *N. f.*

In half sheets sleep idly the weeping
Somewhere the world weeps with you
And if by similar logic,
The world laughs harmoniously,
Smiles, red tints of lips spread,
Breathes or sits awake
Pertaining to the wisps fiddling in and over
The mossy cobblestone bridges
You see, love,
Even when the gods
Lace your eyes with blind configuration
As you're draped down on your bed
With imaginary binds across your chest
Of self love
Someone is capsized the same way
Even across borders
These similarities are what make us
Slightly more bound to each other

$$\sim N.f.$$

Do not tolerate their words
If they do not settle well
In the way they touch your shoulder
That displaces you
Do not fear the urge to walk away

~ N. f.

And with these solemn thoughts
I shall take my leave
For you have over welcoming thoughts
At midnight
And at 4:14
You've tumbled through my memories every night
At 4:14
Yet I don't think you're capable
Of rendering what slashes you've dashed me with
A cacophony of destructive behavior
You cannot comprehend
At 4:14
You are like the cycle of water
Floating at the bottom of my memory
Rising and defying against my heartbeat
Clouding and fogging every crevice along my scalp
Falling back down to drown
With the rest of the poison
Until it is time for you to surface again
At 4:14
I will cross my fingers
You will be able to fall back in line

$$\sim N.f.$$

You reached out to me
I miss you, I really do
But I don't even feel the urge
To tell you anything back
I set myself aside and let myself listen
To the way the universe is calling out
Don't believe him, don't fall for it
And I remember a time where I used to
My lord, I use to fall for these messages every time
But something in this moment
Is a calming breakthrough
Free from the torment
Of cycling back to those who hurt me
 —I have finally learned how to stand up

~ N. f.

In the barrier of the silent sky
If life were to elude is
As the saying goes:
May death do its part
For there must be an ending
To each and every start
In the atmosphere, an upraised faith,
But a real fate,
Defines one day even the clouds
Shall fade
And the world will crack
The stars will dip into our world
And we will know
How it feels
To finally be one
In such an infinite continuum
Oh, how glorious it feels
To start as star dust
And end as it, too

~ *N. f.*

5 : 0 0

Oh how glorious it feels
To start as star dust
And end as it, too

In one embrace
I will reign it all
As my gown
Fury will reign upon
My demons
As they dance inside my soul
To invite every lasting nerve with fury,
With passion,
And with pride
    — Fear doesn't always have to be scary

       ~ *N. f.*

My love,
You brought me love
In the most abandoned of corridors
Handed to me in alley ways
The backs of rooms, street corners
At times when I was overflowing with bliss

I feel as though I have floated
Through all of the borders
And have seen the clouds through planes
I've never rode in
And the words you grant me
Are the paints to the map

You give so much
You travel to mountains, and towers, and countries
To paint more world for me

You bring me the world,
My love,
From the different places in your heart
And sent from the heavens above
You draw in the missing flowers
In the blanks and open spaces
Handing them to me in alley ways

You brought me all of this love

~ N .f.

Madness is only repeating itself
Let me stop the cycle
By letting you free
For I am in grief of not loving
Nature for its course
And it would be wrong of me to act on what nature
Cannot gradually do
I cannot command gravity to pull
Our strings back together
And I most certainly cannot
Create a force to fill this space with,
No more than the sky can
Command the rain to halt
And evaporate again
Madness would be trying to create
Life from a dead thing
And I cannot revive what we once had

$\sim N.f.$

I look into people's eyes
When I speak to them
Their words only speak whispers
When the pigments of their irises
Scream novels

~ *N. f.*

The way you carry yourself
Will define your future
So handle yourself with
Caution
And always love what you hold

~ *N. f.*

My skin stretches beyond
Long curves and folds none have seen
As much as above as beneath
The broken ride's I've traversed
The dreams I am still dreaming
I have this skin that stretches for miles
It's all mine, try as you'd like
To change it
And it's perfectly okay to change yourself
But don't do it for others
As your personality
Is flavor already bursting
From the seams

~ N. f.

My love,
For when I wake up
From a repetitive dream
Of ocean tides that bubble around our toes
And orange sunsets that are gifted
With the ribbon of your soft hands
Laced into mine
A cabana that smiles, veranda doors that open
To us, and a little girl with brown hair
Flying paper planes over the banister railing
With a green eyed boy, rocking back and forth
To the rhythm of the waves catching the stairs
Of his castle he imagines somewhere far away
We put them to rest
Clean sand from the doorway
Dance our way into each other's arms for as long
As the moon holds us
To the end of the shore we will glide
Until your forehead
Leans against mine, and your hands
Cover the sunburns of my shoulders
You cover my eyes,
Whisper my favorite quote softly in my ear
And seal it with a kiss
And when you unveil my eyes
I see my bed sheets and an empty space
To my left
I find myself repeating
I love you
Yet again, every morning

~ N. f.

I love flowers
The pastel stories that are embedded in the rocks
And thrived
For why was such a beauty
Graced upon this world?
Of the infinity lurking beyond in the universe
Why would such a fine craft
Of blooming cells occur to be
An earthly, god given creation?
Or even, perhaps,
Why were we to discover it?
The chance we ourselves bloom here
Makes everything feel as though
Life itself is amicable
Through chances
Through fate
And I love the flowers
Because we were the ones chosen to discover them
Not held in captivity,
But for us to expect the wild
And cherish the precious gifts
This world has held ourselves to find

$\sim N.f.$

All this time
I have finally evolved
There's so much room between us
So I stay and say we meet again

Will you keep to your promise as I keep to mine?

~ N. f.

There's a reason I write
Not for I want to
But I must
Simply because
Of the moments
He took my breath away

…

But I also write
To find sanctuary in the darkness
To belong in a world I love
I write for you, the reader,
To find revelation
And safety within yourself
And hope these words take your hand
And guide you to it

~ N. f.

The connections we find
Are the ones I must write for
To preserve the gold I saw in her smile
To reflect on the journey of his hands
Painting hearts on my back
Tracing stars
On the knobs of my spine
And branches that bend around my shoulder blades
To cling onto
As he pulls me ever so closer
To the way he wished to show me love
For what felt like a lifetime
That impression
Is what I want to reprint
So vividly onto a canvas
Vowels and constants will spur
I write to preserve
The sanction
I found in you
And I found in myself

$\sim N.f.$

7/Un/Open/ned/Let/ters

1/

    You say my eyes once drove you
To the end of the world and could lift up skies
What colors can you make them out to be?
You say your memory falls
To the void,
Like the name of this letter, this heart o' mine
It's hard enough to stand on solid ground
But love, you once whispered to me
It's even harder to reach
I/love/you,/please/reply/
Sincerely,/
Me/

2/

    I sat on the edge of a lighthouse this morning
I can still feel my hand pressed into the bar
It reminds me of how you grabbed my waist
It was cold, only because of the snow
But I recalled your lips, so full of piercing warmth around
That blistering cold
I had almost forgotten it all
Until the simplest of things
Reminded me of you
I/love/you,/please/reply/
Sincerely,/

3/

    Morning coffee never smelled as good as you did
Back in that October haze

With rainbows sprinkling the tips of leaves
That drew up softly arisen eyes
Lips spread wide
I often contemplate the stars
Morning through night
And print our name in more constellations
We could ever fathom
I/love/you,/please/reply

4/

    There! Beyond our beings,
All epithets could never sing
A quiet temptress lays down in the thickets
With her staff laid to rest nearby
If you were to wake her, the earth would unsettle
Beneath her; the ground would sprout her to
The top of the trees
With a thousand doves to break her somber
She would replenish us, however
The white pillars surrounding her
Would never seem to leave
I/love/you,/please/

5/

    I wish I could call upon the most meticulous artist
To invoke my bleeding heart for you
And open it as wide as the sea
For you to gaze upon,
Oh how wonderful!
But a beast has been lurking about
It does not pursue you
But it seems to be here to warn me…

I/love/you,/

6/
    I count what days we miss
I've written so much, but crumpled it all away
For it was all amiss, my love,
I fear for these words don't even reach you
Collectively in my mind, and in my hand,
I give my upmost strength to write you
But I'm shouldered with high tides, paddling for land
When it's you I feel I can't reach for
I seem to be sinking deeper, seething into
The deep everglade sea
I/love/

7/
    I move with the room
That I use to so vividly see you in
Holding linens to a humming that's drowned out
I held my heart open to thoughts
But it's so difficult to write
With half a heart
Eaten by the wolves of the forest
Eyes gouged out by Neptune's spear
And sirens of your presence
There was a skin so foreign in this linen—
In the linen you brought her here
And now my beasts itch
And have come to shred down these empty walls
Look into my burning eyes,
Tell me,
What colors do you see in them now?
I/

8/
    Done, here I leave you
The last note dedicated to you
I hope my beasts bring you as much company
As they brought me

$$\sim N.f.$$

Rest your frosted thighs
On the wooden bench, let the rusted watch
Tick from the handle
And stretch your legs
As I drape my hair on your lap,
I will recite words meticulously to the sky
Before those frosted eyes drip
A blazing storm to come up as the sun wakes in the west
Pick apart the willows as tapestries
Strands of snow to weave and unravel
Peel my skin off as a winter coat
And let it breathe
Underneath the waking spring sun
I wind thin strands over the carcass
As it peacefully basks in the rays
And I kiss its forehead, for I will not return
And this is when you're here
To kiss my hand and keel away
All the bitter winter
And become my hold
Steadfast, we will move forward
And join to one path
Across the amber-rose sun

$\sim N. f.$

I know there's strength
That lies within you
For the years and years
I've searched
I almost forgot to search within me

                    ~ N. f.

Blooming you shall be
Amidst the wine stained bar
Surrounded by beat-less, bloodless boons
You shall remain silent, soft
With a whiskey tapped between your fingernails
As hard as the rocks against the tidal sea
Down, down, drown—drowsy darling
The blood trickles pebbles through your
Watered-down skin
Wising memories could be distanced
As casted fishing lines in the plains of the ocean
Treasures to be hidden, reprised at the seafloor
Here you trace the smudged rim
And ponder the stories
Of midnight fantasies
They bloom, like you,
In the strangest of times
And build them into the most beautiful of things

~ *N. f.*

I will fall
But fall I will unto you

~ N. f.

To me, my work isn't a job
It is a blessing to be a leader
And to guide my students
The path to their dreams
The hundreds of men and women
I surround myself with are here to learn
How to walk their way
To their destinies
I am here
To watch them bloom

~ N. f.

In the time we crave
I pray upon you
To hold your resiliency
Against the red smoke
To find currents in something other
Than beckoning trenches
Praise no other woman
No other woman to be but me
Because my strength will build towers in your foundation
If you lend me the stone
Your sad silence will not be condoned
And this tired stature will be brooding
But tired we will fall into the arms of one another
Tired, yes, but we will grow together

~ N. f.

Draw the light
To your fingertips
And paint stars with it
Lingering bewilderments
Never spoken, yet never forgotten
Whisper all things
That remind you of poetry
The garden escapes of which your heart
Takes your hand and guides you through
The ever-expanding earth
Forever bleeding out new sounds
And listen to it all
Finding yourself will be
Stepping into new shoes
To find the ones that will take you the furthest
For now, fall from the
Teetering cliff to embrace the thought
That your wings
Are authentic, and will catch you
Amidst the plummeting fear
For darling, you must learn that the first step
To recovery is risking it all
Just to soar

~ N. f.

Reposed in the passenger's seat
My denim coat rests on my lap
My heart firm in my hand
Wrapped in velvet nails, the ones you noticed
My eyes gleaming
Like the water you describe from the shores of Florida
Withdrawn into my frame
And the everglade spring I mentioned
Was inside you from Evergreen
What a young adoration we created
In the space of that hot car
It's been a long age
Since I've felt purely encompassed
In my own being
With you,
It made everything brighter
Warmer, calmer, safer, and brighter
It was a start to something new, intriguing,
And I couldn't take enough of it in
I couldn't soak in the warmth of that car
As much as I had hoped
But I knew, deep inside my being
That this would not be the last memory
We would be creating

~ N. f.

Beautiful child,
In the hands of the scattered brokenness
What was wrapped with winter storms
Has dropped into the beating, blessed open
Sunshine presented in the morning
Fresh out of mourning
A strong woman wipes the cold from her rusted cheeks
A body of stars and the delicacy of evergreens

She was able to move onto bigger, better, bolder,
More beautiful things

~ N. f.

6 : 0 0

She moved onto bigger, better, bolder
More beautiful things

It wasn't a man nor woman calling out for her
Present, a silhouette of her
Came the love of herself first

~ N. f.

I will unravel all I am
And look at what's underneath
For I don't need anyone
To do it for me

                ~ N. f.

As if the fence
That stretched to the sky
Was enough to stop her
Proceeding her way
As if the clouds
Were enough to blind her
Watching the sunrise shine
As if the thorns
Prickling her feet as she stepped
Were enough to tear her
From her toxic past
As if the water
That fell through her throat and filled her lungs
Was enough to drown her
As she dove into the deep, independent ocean
As if the limit
Inching a painful speed
Was enough to slow her
Speeding on the empty highway at night
As if the doubt
Everyone said she couldn't do it
So she did it
And
She
Did
It
With
Passion
She flew with wings
Of color

~ N. f.

Age is not a mile marker for wisdom
But the moments in them could be

~ N. f.

The green in your eyes
Dips the constellations
Into dim nights
For you wonder
Why I'm captivated
By their irreplaceable beauty

$\sim N.f.$

I could see
The hues of color spark
Something inside of him
Under the fading sun
With his arm around me
Coyly playing with my hair
As guitar strings to my open heart
I know it's natural to gaze on the beauty
Of the unknown
As long as I can sing
With it as it fades
And lights up in the dawn

~ N. f.

My love,
The candid photos always frame you perfectly
The warmth in your spirit
Does not need change, or to be staged
My love, you do not need an alteration
Of any kind
Because you already hold everything in your palms
My love
You always live in candid moments
I can't save snapshots to my memory
Or upload them to my heart
I'll never find a way to stop loving you
Because I fell in love with you from the very start

~ *N. f.*

I walk besides one million stories
And only one I get to speak
You could be taking your first steps
Through your mother's arms
At twenty years of age
Doddle through her garden and out at thirty
Muster over the fence at fifty four
Meander through the thickets, hazy and wide-eyed
Head hoisted over the bloody headlines
And enough pickets
To reimburse a thousand forest acres
And at seventy
Have made it halfway home for supper
Light pocketed and blundering around the beaten path
Life is so vicariously unappreciated
It's an understatement to say time flies by
Appreciate every sight—every pleasant or not moment
Live a life history books will be thirsty for

$\sim N.f.$

> I will forgive
> But I shall never forget
> The poetry you have instilled in me
> And the importance of love
> I have learned
>
> ~ *N. f.*

A certain season comes to mind
When you cross my thoughts
Sharp winds and crisp auburn leaves
Blue atmosphere—eyes even bluer
Skin bitten softly
Drained by the light in the frosted sun
A brush sculpting the banks of Alaska
Layered on your shoulders
Painted in your hair
In contrast to the iron
Casted in your veins
Cotton wood warped hands
And the birds singing a sweet lullaby

~ N. f.

For one has no purpose
To be entangled with which
Takes away from true entity
Meaningful, deceitful catch
Of which only one can gaze
At the true being behold in front of them
To gaze with wondrous epiphany
But never to grasp, never to hear, nor to attach

~ N. f.

Upon the rooftops
Of orange kissed light
He twisted strands of my hair between his fingertips

So strange to find
Two humans sitting in a world
They have yet to understand

~ N. f.

Burn,
She whispered
As she watched her sorrow
Crumble to ash

~ N. f.

To the limitless
The sky won't be your barrier

To the falling
It's alright to plummet sometimes

To the sometimes
Know you weren't best to be their always

To the always
You find your ways to hide and seek

To the seekers
Keep on reaching

To the reachers
Take what is yours to keep

To the keepers
One day someone will truly grasp your love

To the lovers
Let your journey test the limits

To the limitless

~ N. f.

For you
A harmoniuos love
Is in a world full of
Loveless droughts

~ N. f.

In these pages
You cannot silence my voice
You cannot destroy my creation
You cannot defend all your lies and rumors
You created about me
You cannot defy against my wrath
You cannot touch me
You cannot carve your fingers into my gold
You will not take their haven
You will not destroy my story
You will not destroy their sanction
You cannot destroy us
You cannot destroy us
You cannot destroy us
And there's *nothing* I won't do
To try and stop you

$\sim N.f.$

And I love
Without faltering tiptoes
Out of the window
Perched upon the shingles
Of the morning bathed in a
Bubbling spring

And I love
The sweet smell of budding orchids
The leather seat
Him handing me the white lovelies
Reprised on my shelf
Where they, too, can feel the springtime kiss
Sweet, welcoming,
Like how he is

And I love
For not loving this morning
Would be a falter
For the beauty in its essence
Reminds me
Of all that I love him for
As he loves me

~ N. f.

With all my spirit,
I will linger towards
A typewriter tapping
To soft sips of caffeine
For falling in love is not to be heartbreaking
But breathtaking

~ N. f.

You can start two hundred letters
In two hundred different ways
Kiss someone in four hundred
That are never the same
Watch the rain fall
From thousands of places
Drag fingers along the skin
Of a dozen different faces
Dance a quarter million minutes
All in different paces
Stare into a billion eyes
Leave just as many traces
Visit all seven continents
In just one decade
Listen to every ounce of music
That breathes through every age
With all this time
To do our people things
Harnessing the power
To notice every last breath
And lead us to our departure
In our century
We learn to smile for what we have left

~ N. f.

This woman
This woman is stronger
Than the hardest of titanium swords
Wielded through battle
And nothing can excuse you
For putting her up
And expecting her to owe you
Like your kindness was a favor
She needed to involuntarily repay

~ N. f.

I fathom the adventures we conjure up
In the morning, sleepy yet alive
With passion and pride that one day
They will no longer just be dreams

~ N. f.

I let my spirit wander
For the best fantasies
Seem to be the ones you
Stumble upon at midnight
Where the moonlight
Filters curiously downward
Where the slitted sheets of frost creep
Along the edge of your bed sheets

~ N. f.

What I plan on doing
Is getting tangled in fairy lights
As they string up the constellations
Taking handfuls of snow
They drip stars
Frostbitten and fuzzy
Down my wrists, absorbed by the bone
Devouring every last flake until
They are one with me
The knuckles of my spine elongate
As I lace my fingers and drowsily
Crack the late nights from the cartilage
Feeling it drain through my toes
I plan on smiling through every waking tear
Every lasting razor sharp burn to my heart
Is a feather I blow gently away

~ N. f.

Lie down
Let the shadows swallow you
Let the terror of the dark sky
Consume and be the only thing around your body
As you imagine yourself the moon
Count the craters that patch your lungs
Watch the beat rise and fall
Your chest becoming two vessels,
Floating, falling
Your eyes astronauts
Exporing every bit of your surface
Diving deeper to reveal what's
Underneath the milky texture of your forearms
Tracing down your torso
Cascading over your thighs
Make your mark on the spots that shine
And venture to the darkest depths
Let it be known
You are the beauty of the night

~ N. f.

Risen from the embers of nightfall
Like a phoenix
Drawn from its own flame
The amber star awakes its golden eyes
The new day is among the dew
Of risen tendrils
Sunflower-kissed faces that call
To the sunlight as easily
As it climbs over the bounty
Skin retakes its branches as they sprout
Roots, emblems and sonnets
And him,
Yes, he who grows the daisies
Into white roses—yet finds all beautiful—
Combs my roots into
Pretty little epithets—
Rather seldom lets beauty lie
In messy entanglements—
With a gaze as deep as the
Midnight forest itself

~ N. f.

Lovers rise, lovers sleep
Of morning rise, the fat moon falls

~ N. f.

I am simply taken
By the sound my soul makes
When I think of you
All the poetry
All the epithets
I write come purely
From the river of my skin
Always circling back to you
So when I become older
The faint trickles of young love
Will be fresh drippings
To continue circling back—
Always back to you

~ N. f.

I love so hard
Because I choose to never live
In a world
Of less love, gratitude, and appreciation
Than I can virtually give

                ~ N. f.

It took so long to teach myself
How to love my body
My thoughts
My actions and accomplishments
Now I'm going to teach you
That *everything* you are doing
Is an act of strength
And beauty
And power
And it is authentically you
No one can take that away

～ *N. f.*

I feel alive
With the way the electricity
Reverberates,
I can connect my bones
Revise the burnt nerves
Rejuvenate my blood
And spark my lungs
From it's depressed, drowsy date
With death
I find my power
Is now breathless
I can feel the lightning
In my soul
And how had it not surfaced before?
Darling,
I believe I felt it
So I opened my chest
And let it rise

~ N. f.

He stopped, pondering
In the middle of the midnight storm
And said,
Kiss me in the rain darling

~ N. f.

You have dreams wild child
Don't let them be
It's that young love wild child
Young love that'll set you free

~ *N. f.*

I still see your silhouette present
In the crevices of this house
The sweet light pouring in
Over your golden hair
I can vividly watch your hand
Comb the roots back
Tucked, but not behind your ear—
You always despised that—
I can feel the air now
Pressed on my chest from the vents
As you turned the street to a place
When were could be alone
I remember the grin spreading my lips
The way your hair felt like silk
Running between my fingers
And the warmth of your breath
On my blushing cheeks
I see and remember the past
As if it were still in motion
Replaying multitudes of moments
Where I could have you again
Again, when you were mine
    —The sweet times I remember

                    ~ N. f.

To her—
To all of the love letters left unseen
To the wrecked and the reckless
The unawake dragon, regal and keep
To her—
Let your beast be reminded
Of the power each breath it distills
Amongst the silent
Wonder of your stare

~ N. f.

The perfect harmony comes
With lots of practice, patience, and time
Don't let anything get in the way of your masterpiece

~ N. f.

Your heart is a wonder
Cherish every emotion
As if it were the last
No matter how small,
How short it feels—
Take it with security
And fasten it close
    —Let every emotion be a lesson

~ N. f.

Arise in the midst of war
May hands untie
Wonderful sanction in the rising smoke
Sunlight filtering through the weeds
Like newborn snakes
Wriggling to free lands

Arise from the den
Of mama's palms and stretch
Those dreary eyes to the horizon
Painted specially for you

Arise like the havens
Calling upon an angel to return home
Welcomed with dreamy arms
And sparkling pathways to guide you
As a shepard does its kin

Arise shall the world
And so shall you

~ N. f.

I didn't believe I would be able to climb this high
Ever in my lifetime
To let myself sit upon my own world
And let me admire the work
And the hardships
And the endless situations
That almost ended in catastrophe
I am here to say that I have not fallen to my doom
Quite yet
That I am still going on proudly
And that no matter what will come my way
I will be able to conquer it
And lead the world
And so will you

$\sim N.f.$

I lay the sweatshirt down
Without a kiss goodnight
The memories are locked,
As his smell is,
In the seams for tonight
Befallen, love,
Hum a sweet song to null
Yourself a humbling rest
Float gently, gently afloat
In your sweetest of dreams
Sweetest of moments will come
And may you wake revitalized

~ N. f.

*It's okay. You will be able to heal.
I believe in you.
This is not the ending of your story,
It is only the beginning.*

Printed in Poland
by Amazon Fulfillment
Poland Sp. z o.o., Wrocław